NATIONAL GEOGRAPHIC
School Publishin

Say Cheese!

PATHFINDER EDITION

By Susan Halko

CONTENTS

Say Cheese!

By Susan Halko

Mild or sharp, creamy or crumbly—there are many kinds of cheese. In fact, there are hundreds of different cheeses from all around the world.

All of these cheeses begin with the same ingredient—milk. But how can you start with milk and end up with so many different kinds of cheese?

Science can help explain. As milk gets made into cheese, it goes through some big changes—**chemical changes**.

Two Ways to Change

Like everything else that takes up space and has mass, milk and cheese are matter. Matter can come in three different states—solid, liquid, and gas.

You probably know that water can be a liquid (drink), a solid (ice), and a gas (water vapor).

When water changes from one state to another, it goes through a physical change. It can change from solid to liquid to gas again and again. Water, ice, and water vapor are all made of the same thing—water!

But cheese is different. It's not just solid milk—it's a whole new substance. And once you have cheese, you can't change it back into milk.

This means that chemical changes are happening to the cheese. Let's find out what causes the chemical changes in cheese making.

From Liquid to Solid

The first step in making cheese is to turn milk into a solid. To do this, cheese makers add bacteria to the milk. Bacteria are tiny living things. They are so small that a million of them would fit on the period at the end of this sentence.

The milk and bacteria are stirred and heated. The bacteria become more active in warmer temperatures. They change the sugar, or lactose, in the milk into lactic acid. Lactic acid is what changes the milk into a solid. It makes the milk look and feel like yogurt. That's a chemical change!

Next, cheese makers add something called rennet to the milk. Rennet is an **enzyme** found in cows' stomachs. It helps speed up the chemical change that is happening. It makes the milk thicker, like pudding.

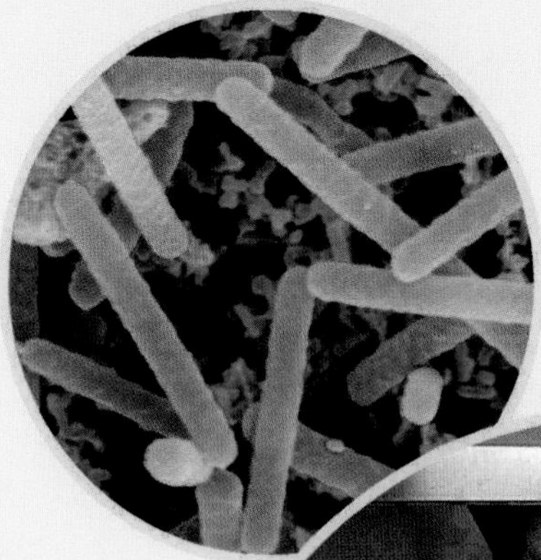

Lactobacilli bacteria are added to milk to make cheese.

The milk is stirred while it is heated.

Curds and Whey

The solid milk, or curd, sits in a watery liquid. This liquid is called whey. It is made of water, extra fat, and protein. The next step is to separate the whey from the curds.

After the whey is gone, some kinds of cheese are packed into molds and dumped in a salt bath. Some, like mozzarella, are reheated and stirred more. This makes the mozzarella stretchy and stringy.

The whey is in liquid form. It is drained out from the curds in a tub like this one.

Cheddar the Cheese

Other kinds of cheese, such as cheddar, are cut into slabs. The slabs are stacked on top of each other and flipped every 15 minutes. This helps drain off more of the whey.

After a lot of stacking and flipping, the slabs are much thinner. They are cut into small pieces and salted. This stacking, flipping, and cutting is called cheddaring.

Cutting the curds into small pieces is an example of a physical change.

Aging

The last step of making cheese takes patience—waiting for the cheese to age. Aging can take weeks, months, or years. The amount of time depends on the type of cheese and the taste wanted. To age properly, cheeses are usually kept in rooms that have controlled temperature and moisture. Too much cold or heat, or too much wetness or dryness, could cause problems.

Some cheeses are wrapped in cloth or dipped in wax. Some are washed in olive oil or another solution while they age.

What about the bacteria? They are still alive in the cheese! They continue to cause changes as cheese ages. These chemical changes affect the cheese's flavor and texture as it ages. The more a cheese ages, the sharper its flavor.

This cheddaring process is used on other types of cheese besides cheddar. For example, it's also used on Derby and Cheshire cheeses.

Few Steps, Many Cheeses

All cheeses follow the same basic steps, but many changes can be made along the way to make different kinds of cheese.

Even the same kind of cheese can be made to have a different taste or texture. This is where the art of cheese making comes into play.

For example, thousands of different bacteria can be added to the milk. Cheese makers decide which ones to use for different kinds of cheese.

They also decide how much whey to drain, what temperatures to use, or whether or not to reheat the curds.

The milk makes a big difference, too. Different breeds of cows make different milk with different qualities. Ever heard of goat cheese? Milk from goats, sheep, and even buffalo can also be used to make different tastes and textures.

Let's check out some of the changes used to make a few famous cheeses.

Limburger cheese

Swiss cheese

Stinky Cheese

Have you ever smelled stinky cheese? The odor can knock your socks off! In fact, some say it smells like sweaty socks.

That's because some bacteria in stinky cheeses are the same bacteria found in human sweat! P.U.!

The rinds, or coverings, of stinky cheeses are washed in different mixtures. This also helps cause the strong smell. You can tell a cheese is stinky if it has an orange rind.

But don't let the smell scare you away. Surprisingly, some stinky cheeses, such as Limburger, have a very mild taste.

Holey Bacteria!

What makes the holes in Swiss cheese? Gassy bacteria. A few weeks after Swiss cheese is made, cheese makers put it in a warm room. When these bacteria are warmed up, they make gas bubbles. Another chemical change!

Swiss cheese is bendable. It curves around the gas bubbles, and this makes the holes in the cheese.

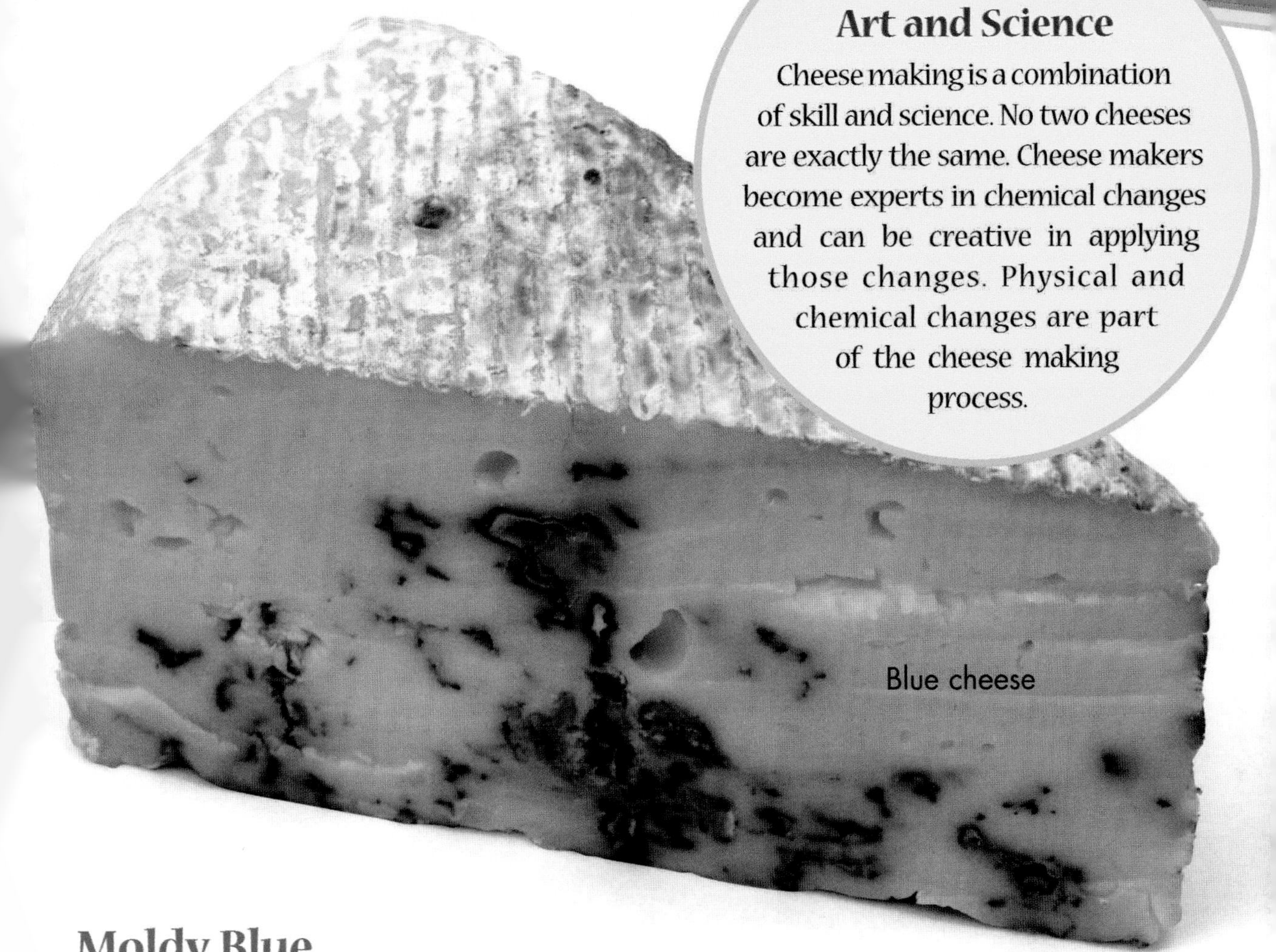

Blue cheese

Art and Science

Cheese making is a combination of skill and science. No two cheeses are exactly the same. Cheese makers become experts in chemical changes and can be creative in applying those changes. Physical and chemical changes are part of the cheese making process.

Moldy Blue

What makes blue cheese blue? Mold! Mold is a kind of fungus. It's added to the milk at the beginning of the process.

As the cheese cools, the mold reacts to the oxygen in the air. The outside of the cheese turns blue. That's a chemical change!

But how does it get the blue lines on the inside? Cheese makers pierce holes in the cheese. Oxygen makes its way inside the holes. Wherever the oxygen goes, the mold turns blue. That's another chemical change!

Wordwise

chemical change: a change in matter that forms a new substance with different properties

enzyme: a substance in plants or animals that speeds up chemical reactions

matter: anything that takes up space and has mass

physical change: when matter changes to look different but does not become a new kind of matter

Changes for Breakfast

Chemical and physical changes happen all the time—even during breakfast!

Let's take a look at a special breakfast menu. It will help you learn about physical and chemical changes that occur while certain foods are made.

But first, review these hints about physical and chemical changes.

Some signs that a chemical change has happened:

- Light or heat is given off
- The color changes
- Bubbling, or gas forms
- The odor or smell changes
- A solid forms
- The change cannot be reversed

Some signs that a physical change has happened:

- The substance is the same; only its properties have changed

Good Morning!

Veggie Omelets

Melting butter in a skillet .... physical change

The butter changes from a solid to a liquid, but it is still the same substance.

Shredding cheese .... physical change

The cheese changes its form, but it's still made of the same stuff.

Chopping the veggies .... physical change

The physical properties of the vegetables changed. They are just smaller pieces. No new substance was made.

Cooking the eggs .... chemical change

The eggs turn from liquid to solid. You can't reverse this change.

Pancakes

Heating the batter .... chemical change

The batter changes from a liquid or goopy substance to a solid or firm pancake. You cannot change the pancakes back into pancake batter.

Side Orders

Toast .... chemical change

Heat makes the bread turn brown and crispy. It smells good!

Cold cereal .... physical change

Adding milk to cereal makes it mushy, but it doesn't make it into a new substance.

Physical and Chemical Changes

Find out what you learned about changes in matter.

1. What is an example of a chemical change in cheese making?
2. What is an example of a physical change in cheese making?
3. Why does Swiss cheese have holes?
4. Why do stinky cheeses smell so bad?
5. Is making waffles a physical change or a chemical change? Explain.